AN ECLECTIC EYE

Selected photographs of TW Murphy

Text by Bob Montgomery

Dreoilín

Published and distributed by Dreoilín Specialist Publications Limited, Tankardstown, Garristown, County Meath, Ireland.
Telephone: (00353) 1 8354481

e-mail: info@dreoilin.ie
First published in March 2014
Photographic Copyright © 2014 The heirs of TW Murphy
Text Copyright © 2014 Bob Montgomery

ISBN 978-1-902773-30-8
A CIP record is available for this title from the British library.
Design by Alan Pepper Design. Set in Bembo by Alan Pepper Design and printed in the Republic of Ireland by Walsh Colour Print.

See our full range of books at:
www.dreoilin.ie

FOREWORD

When Tom and David Murphy made me aware that they had a number of albums of photographs taken by their grandfather, TW Murphy, I looked forward with eager anticipation to seeing them, knowing that 'TWM' had been a pivotal figure in the recording of early cycling and motorcycling in Ireland.

Indeed, from the 1890s through to the early 1950s 'TWM' had been present at all of the important events in Irish motorsport and had recorded many of them in *The Irish Cyclist* and *The Motor News,* both publications with which he was long associated. However, I did not anticipate that his photographs would also bear witness to many of the great events between 1909 and 1916 when the majority of these photographs were taken. Looking through the photographs I found myself transported to a new understanding of life in Ireland in these years, particularly in relation to the Royal visit of 1911 and the events of Easter week 1916.

The photographs of TWM (as he was invariably known) give a new insight into both these events as well as other happenings of that time including the Dublin to Belfast air race of 1912 and Hawker's crash at Loughshinny in 1913 as well as valuable insights into everyday life in Ireland. A child of the great cycling boom of the 1880s, its natural that this pastime features strongly in his photographs, reflecting the huge social change that cycling brought about in Irish society through the freedom that it provided for its followers to explore hitherto inaccessible horizons as well as allowing an interaction between the sexes that had not existed previously.

TWMs photographs have a spontaneity and candidness that is rare for the time as well as a technical accomplishment that is very impressive. Although we don't know when he began taking photographs – or what camera equipment he used - the earliest of the albums displays all the hallmarks of a beginner but clearly he learned fast as the other albums show an understanding of good photography that few achieve.

I hope, like me, you will be transported back to another Ireland, of momentous days and ordinary days, on which TW Murphy's wonderful photographs throw new light.

Bob Montgomery

TW MURPHY - A LIFE LIVED FULLY

Tomas W Murphy was born in 1872 and died in 1953. His eighty-one years encompassed the coming of the automobile, the invention of the aeroplane and two World Wars, as well as revolution, the golden age of touring and great social change in his native Ireland.

When Tom was born at Marlborough Street, Dublin, on 12th January 1872, life in the second city of the empire could be precarious. His brother John was born two years later but the whole family, mother, father and two boys, were hospitalised in the Adelaide Hospital with Scarlatina in 1879. Sadly, his brother John and his mother succumbed to the illness. Their deaths were to mark a sea change in Tom's life. Two years later his father also died and Tom entered St. Peter's Parish School for orphan boys as a paying boarder.

In 1884 Tom attended his first Athletic and Cycling Sports Caledonian Games at Lansdowne Road and perhaps inspired by what he had seen, bought his first bicycle. A year later, in 1885, Tom left school and entered the Inland Revenue Service at an initial salary of 6/- per week. Sometime in 1888, he saw Dunlop's pneumatic tyre in Belfast and with an ever-growing interest in cycling matters, he took a major step at Easter 1892 when he left the Inland Revenue Service and joined the staff, "in a very junior capacity", of *The Irish Cyclist* (at a salary of £1-5s-0d per week). Having joined the Irish Road Club (IRC) in 1891 (founded a year earlier in 1890) by now he was also competing in cycle events and the same year saw him place 3rd in his first long distance cycle race – 116 miles from Dublin to Limerick. More success followed in 1893 when he won the Irish Road Club 100 mile handicap race around the Mourne Mountains. His prize was a Swift bicycle that he promptly exchanged for a tricycle.

RJ Mecredy, the well known cyclist, who was to play such an important role in TWM's life, formed a new company in 1894 to publish The Irish Cyclist, having taken full control of the publication from it's founder. TWM was to be a key, if not arguably the key person in it's publication and also in due course, that of it's sister publication introduced in 1900, The Motor News. That year, 1894, was also probably the height of TWM's cycle racing career and chief among his successes were setting a new 100 miles, 12 hour record on a Humber

TWM enjoyed cycle touring throughout his life. This photograph was taken, presumably by his wife Annie, during one of their tandem tours in Wales.

bicycle covering a distance of 196 miles and 6 perches; winning the IRC London Tandem Bicycle Race with HO Binns on a Swift and also winning the North Cycle Club's Tricycle Race on a Swift Tricycle partnered also by HE Binns. Their record of 356 ½ miles in sixteen hours was not beaten until 1915 when HG Cooke achieved 360 ½ miles.

On St. Stephen's Day 1895 TWM became engaged to Annie Jane Allen, while earning 25 shillings per week. He then attended the IRC social gathering at Rostrevor where he

The Murphy family on their first car, a Rover 6 hp, in 1905.

purchased a split second watch at the very considerable cost of £42.10.0. (TWM recorded this watch stolen in London in 1935).

On 17th June 1896 Annie and TWM were married in St. Thomas' Church, Cathal Brugha Street, Dublin, by Rector J Pearson. The couple honeymooned in North Wales by tandem and upon their return moved to number 34 Xavier Avenue, North Strand, at a rent of £24 per annum.

This was a key year for motorists with the introduction in November of the Motor Car Act that gave motorists freedom from the need to be preceded by a person walking and carrying a red flag. Motorists in Britain celebrated Emancipation Day by driving from London to Brighton and back. As TWM recalled in The Motor News in 1938: "As cycling journalists, we were more interested in bicycles than these new-fangled horseless vehicles, but each of us had a commission to 'cover' the Emancipation Day Run for a daily newpaper. We were assigned seats on an MMC dogcart. Between London and Croydon it stopped frequently; at Croydon it gave up the ghost. I was unperturbed; I felt I had already collected enough material to write more about how motor cars behaved than any editor would print".
(Invited to participate in the 1938 event forty-two years later he missed the start and his ride on a Daimler. Travelling by train to Brighton he managed to meet up with the Daimler and returned to London on it, a drive he enjoyed very much).
The following year,1897 was a red-letter year with the birth of his first child, William Allen. Also in that year, together with John Kyle, he undertook a tandem tour to Killarney, possibly to coincide with the visit there of the Prince of Wales (later King George V).

TWM was meticulous in recording the events of his life, even to the extent of recording his 'first glasses' in 1898. In that year he also recorded another tandem tour with Annie to Killarney, on this occasion in the company of a Mr. and Mrs. Smith.

1903 was of course the year of the Irish Gordon Bennett Race around a figure eight course based on Athy in County Kildare. Tom was Head Timekeeper at the Athy Control, assisting like many Irish motoring enthusiasts in the successful running of this important race. TWM recalled in later years the thrill of being driven around the course by Bob Poole, a pioneer motorist from Tullamore, on his De Dion. The Irish race is widely regarded as the event that made the Irish public 'car conscious'. Before the race there were probably no more that between fifty and one hundred cars in the whole island of Ireland. By year-end that figure had risen to around 1,500. TWM was not one to be left behind and acquired his first car, a Rover 6 hp in 1905 for £130, writing about his experiences with it in the issue of The Motor News dated 22nd September 1906.

The Ariel Cup won outright by TWM.

By 1904 his journalistic career had blossomed and as well as the Mecredy publications his writings appeared in *The Irish Times, Belfast Telegraph, the Weekly Irish Times, The Freeman's Journal* and *Ireland's Saturday Night* in addition to the more specialist journals, the *Motor Cycle Journal, the Motor Cycle, Motoring Illustrated, Car* and *Autocar.* No doubt it was the income so derived that enabled him to enjoy a motorcycle holiday in France that summer. On the sporting side he was the only rider to manage to complete the entire route of the Two Hundred Miles Non-stop Trial for the Ariel Cup without a stop. The course had taken the riders from Dublin to Waterford, via Naas, Castledermot, Carlow and Thomastown and back to the city boundary. A maximum speed limit of twenty miles per hour and a minimum of fifteen were required. The only maintenance allowed to the machines was refilling with oil and spirit during the compulsory stop of one hour prior to the return leg. TWM rode a 3 hp Singer motorcycle and gained the gold medal for his performance. He also found time to act as Chief Timekeeper and Starter at the IAC Speed Trials held on the Velvet Strand,

In 1904 TWM acted as Chief Timekeeper and Starter at the IAC Speed Trials on the Velvet Strand, Portmarnock. Here he is about to give the signal to start to two competiors.

Portmarnock. The following year (1905) TWM did it again, in the process winning the Ariel Cup outright. Once again he was the sole rider to complete the course non-stop – an outstanding achievement. (The richly ornamented Ariel Cup TWM received, that the family donated, is displayed today in the Clubhouse of the Royal Irish Automobile Club in Dawson Street, Dublin). In that same year he recorded joining the Irish Automobile Club (later the Royal Irish Automobile Club), paying a fee of £3 and 3 shillings. Evidently, he found this sum excessive and did not rejoin until 1950.

His Rover 6 hp was replaced with an 8 hp model in 1907 and in 1908, in a sign of his growing financial security, he purchased numbers 7 and 8 Beachfield Terrace, Clontarf, and moved into number 8. (This was later renamed and renumbered as number 48 Vernon

Avenue). In July, a second son, Thomas Desmond, was born and in 1908, Allen, now aged 12 made his parents proud by taking first place in Ireland in his school examinations at Mountjoy School.

Having exchanged two wheels for four TWM entered in the Irish Reliability Trials organized by the IAC in June 1906 in his 6 hp Rover. Reliability Trials became very important to motor manufacturers at this time as a means to demonstrate the reliability and achievement of their products. The Irish and Scottish events became the most important and drew large entries of both private and professional drivers. All of the major makes of car were represented and these events were a difficult test of car and driver. Each car carried an 'Observer' and marks were lost for any unscheduled stops and any deviations from the proscribed route. In 1906, the event started from the Clubhouse of the IAC in Dawson Street, Dublin, and proceeded over four days to Carlow and back (Day 1); Dublin to Dundalk and back (Day 2); Dublin to Gorey and back (Day 3) and Dublin to Newtownmountkennedy and back (Day 4). For his efforts TWM was awarded a coveted Gold Medal in his class, a considerable achievement, not least to one so relatively new to driving.

Having exchanged his 6 hp Rover for an 8 hp model he returned to the event in 1907. Over a longer route the 1907 event did not favour TWM who retired on the second day for reasons unknown. In the 1908 event (by which time the route was taking the competitors around the whole of Ireland) he again finished creditably but the following year was listed as one of the official timekeepers on the event. This was the end of the series of IAC Irish Reliability Trials apart from a short lived attempt to revive them as a Light Car Trial in 1914.

Sometime around 1908 and 1909 TWM evidently acquired a camera, make unknown, and began to take the photographs that are the subject of this book.

His earliest photographs were, as one would expect, amateurish, but unlike the majority of amateur photographers, TWM soon improved to the extent that his photographs became important records of the events he attended, often on behalf of his employers. One of the most significant of these events was the royal visit to Ireland of the newly crowned King George V in 1911. TWM's photographs of the visit are unique and the excited crowds on

Driving his 6 hp Rover, TWM won a Gold Medal in the 1906 IAC Irish Reliability Trial. He takes a break while waiting for one of the tests to begin.

the streets of Dublin stand in contrast to the destruction he was to photograph just five years later in the aftermath of the Sinn Fein Rising.

A new Douglas motorcycle and sidecar was acquired in 1912 and in 1913 he attended a Napier Trial in the Dolomites. This event was to be repeated in 1914 but preparations had to be abandoned because of the outbreak of the First World War. Still passionately interested in motorcycling, TWM was a founder member of the Motor Cycle Union of Ireland (MCUI). He served as Southern Centre President for the first time in 1912 – something he was to do again in 1916, 1917, 1918, 1932, 1934, 1935 and 1943. In addition he was President of the MCUI in 1923, 1935 and 1943.

The outbreak of the Easter Rising at Easter 1916 brought TWM onto the streets of Dublin to record events with his camera. The premises of Mecredy, Percy & Company Limited at

34 Lower Abbey Street were destroyed and their records lost. Despite this, RJ Mecredy & Percy published a booklet* of his photographs and more of his photographs also appeared in at least two other publications and a number of books.

Representing the Irish Times he accompanied other journalists on a visit to the Belgian War Fronts in 1918 and later that year, lost his friend Joe Bradley when a submarine in the Irish Sea sank the MV Leinster.

In 1907, TWM drove his newly acquired 8 hp Rover in the IAC Irish Reliability Trial, but sadly retired on the second day of the event.

April 1924 brought news of the death of RJ Mecredy at a sanatorium in Drumfires, Scotland. 'Arjay' had been in ill health for some time and TWM wrote a lengthy obituary in the Motor News, 'RJ Mecredy As I Knew Him'. It's a fascinating piece that runs to four and a half pages of the magazine, in the process almost revealing as much about it's author as it does about Mecredy. Never one to pull punches, TWM's fondness for Arjay is apparent but that does not prevent him mentioning how difficult it was to obtain an increase in salary from him. TWM's obituary of RJ Mecredy is particularly important because more than anything else written about him it gives us a realistic pen portrait of this seminal figure in the development of cycling and motoring in Ireland. "I have lived", he wrote, " to see pass away the man who influenced my whole life more than any other!"

Just four years later, JC Percy, who had been first Mecredy's rival as editor of *The Irish Wheelman,* and then from mid-1903 on his business partner, died. TWM meanwhile, had made his first trip to Canada (where his daughter Dorothy now lived) and the USA. In June 1931 he left Mecredy Percy. He was to return to Mecredy Percy in 1935, when EJ Mecredy, Arjay's son, left to take up a post in the Royal Irish automobile Club. Shortly afterwards he

* *'Dublin after the Six Days Insurection.'*

was joined by Athol Harrison, who would succeed him as editor at the Motor News (The Irish Cyclist had ceased publication in 1929). Athol Harrison is today fondly remembered in the world of Irish motorsport as the doyen of handicappers and timekeepers.

A move to Rathfarnham in 1930 saw him leave Clontarf where he had lived for about thirty years and where he had brought up his family. A few years before, in 1932 he and Annie had become grandparents to Allen's first born, Thomas Desmond, who was born in October of that year in the town of March in Cambridgeshire. He traveled to Paris with EJ Mecredy to attend the bi-annual conference of the Federation Internationale Des Clubs Motorcyclists and shortly before war was declared he bought a 10 hp Hillman.

Apart from his many other interests, TWM had joined the Institute of Journalists in 1903 and was elected a Fellow in 1928. He was to hold every office in the Dublin and Irish District that it was possible for him to hold over a period of forty years – a remarkable record – and took great interest in the orphan fund, no doubt remembering his own difficult early circumstances. During the Second World War he was selected for the specially created office of Deputy for the President of the Institute in Ireland, an honour that gave him great pleasure. In later years, a former past president of the Institute, J Murray Watson from Edinburgh, recalled a visit to Ireland in 1948 when TWM had taken charge of him and his wife. Visiting the Book of Kells in Trinity College both men were so taken up in its splendor that they failed to notice the time passing until they suddenly realized they were going to be at least fifteen minutes late for an interview with the President of Ireland, Sean T O'Kelly, at his residence in Dublin's Phoenix Park.

> "We were hurriedly ushered into the reception room and as soon as the attendant had gone to inform the President of our arrival, TWM, quick as lightning, darted to the mantelpiece and turned back the hands of the clock a quarter of an hour. In came the President and we sat chatting with him until eventually he took out his gold watch, presumably as a hint to us that time was up. As he did so his eye caught the mantelpiece clock and a look of bewilderment came across his face, although he made no remark about the discrepancy. Before saying goodbye he took us out to the grounds to show us some trees that had been planted by British Royalties in the former days, and as he re-entered the house the last I saw of him was having another look at his watch".

By the end of the Second World War, TWM was 73 and at an age when most men thought

TWM speaking at an event to celebrate the success of Reg Armstrong in the Isle of Man TT Race. From left is Fred Armstrong, Reg Armstrong and Reg's mother, Mag.

of retirement. He continued to work as hard as ever contributing to several publications but particularly the *Irish Independent*. He travelled every year to the Isle of Man TT Races, having only missed one year since the race was inaugurated, and continued to work on behalf of the MCUI and the Institute of Journalists. In June of 1946 he and Annie celebrated their golden wedding anniversary and he continued to take an annual holiday in Britain.

But time was taking it's toll and the early years of the 1950s saw him in failing health, culminating in his death on 9th June 1953 at the age of 82. He was followed by Annie just seven months later when she died in February 1954.

For Derek

Dara Residential Services is based in Celbridge in North Kildare and supports people with intellectual disabilities to live in ordinary houses and to get involved in the local community. Dara also provides regular breaks-from-home for people living with their families. Through its independent service brokerage programme, *possibilitiesplus,* Dara supports individuals to develop their unique living arrangements.
A donation from the sale of each book is being made to Dara Residential Services.

IT'S THE POSTMAN!

The Murphy girls encounter a bowler-hatted postman outside their house in Clontarf. The postal system using stamps was introduced in Britain and Ireland in 1840 with the introduction of the world's first adhesive postage stamp, the Penny Black. Prior to that a postal system had existed in Ireland since the late sixteenth and early seventeenth centuries.

ANNIE JANE MURPHY

Annie Jane Murphy, TW Murphy's long suffering wife, whom he married in 1896. He claimed she often regretted being married to a journalist. Nevertheless, she was his devoted companion on numerous cycle tours in Ireland and abroad often sharing a tandem cycle, and belieing her frail appearance. Annie Murphy died aged 87 in February 1954, just seven months after her husband.

STEPPING OUT

The family of TW Murphy set out from their home at 8 Beachfield Terrace (48 Vernon Avenue) in Clontarf, most likely for Church. The girls, from left to right, Olive, Gladys and Dorothy, wear expressions displaying differing attitudes ranging from nonchalance to bemusement at their father, the photographer, while brother Allen is distracted as mother Annie shepherds them along.

MERCER'S SCHOOL, CASTLEKNOCK

TW Murphy's daughters, Dorothy and Olive, attended Mercer's School at Castleknock. What makes this photograph particularly interesting is the Teddy Bear. Teddy Bears were only just coming into widespread popularity when this photograph was taken around 1909. It's the earliest photograph I've come across showing a Teddy Bear in Ireland. Dorothy is seated in the centre of the front row.

DUBLIN ZOO

A delightful photograph of two of the Murphy girls riding a baby elephant at Dublin's famous Zoo. Such rides were a feature of the Zoo in days gone by and the editor can recall such events in his youth.

THE HIBERNIAN MARINE SCHOOL

Founded in 1766 as a charitable School and Institution to *"Maintain, clothe and educate the orphans and children of mariners who had either perished or were worn out in the service of the King or the Merchant Service."* For many years the school was in Ringsend, then at Sir John Rogerson's Quay until 1872, later at 1 Upper Merrion Street, at Grove House, Rathmines, and finally in 1904 to this fine red sandstone building (now demolished) at Seafield Road, Clontarf.

A feature of the school was the naval uniform worn by boarding pupils. Twice on Sundays the boys of the school marched military fashion the short distance from the school to church services at St. John the Baptist Church of Ireland on Seafield Road. In T W Murphy's photograph they are crossing the junction of Seafield Road with Vernon Avenue. Allen is nearest the camera on the front row.

LEOPARDSTOWN AVIATION MEETING 1910

Just eight months after the first flight in Ireland, the Irish Aero Club organised Ireland's first Aviation Meeting at Leopardstown racecourse. The Irish Aero Club had been formed by an initative of the members of the Irish Automobile Club in November 1909.

The Bleriot monoplane of J Armstrong Drexel is readied for flight at Leopardstown. The Bleriot employed wing warping rather than ailerons as can be clearly seen here and looks well used. Drexel, an American, had learned to fly at Claude Graham White's School at Pau, France, in 1909.

Cecil Grace prepares to take a lady passanger for a short flight around Leopardstown. Both Cecil Grace and Armstrong Drexel gave a number of 'joy-rides' during the event.

A delightful photograph of Cecil Grace about to take a
lady passenger aloft on his Farman biplane during the
Leopardstown Aviation Meeting. Passenger comforts
look pretty rudimentary considering the cost of a short
'hop' at £10. Grace's parents had emigrated from Ireland
to America , becoming American citizens, before settling
in Chile, where Cecil was born. Cecil learned to fly in
England in 1909.

Airborne! The Farman biplane of Cecil Grace
takes to the air. While rudimentary, like other
aircraft of this period, the Farman was a rugged
and reliable performer.

A curious spectator casts his eye over the engine mounting
and undercarriage mechanism of Drexel's Bleriot monoplane.
The Gnome rotary engine can be clearly seen. In the Spring
of 1910 Drexel had established an aerodrome at Beaulieu in
Hampshire.

The Lord Lieutenant of Ireland and his wife, Lord and Lady Aberdeen, were amongst the visitors to the Leopardstown Aviation Meeting. Lady Aberdeen was a Scottish author and an advocate of women's rights.

CYCLE RACING AT BALRATH CROSS

The Post Office at Balrath Cross on the road between Ashbourne and Slane was a popular turning point for cycle races originating in Dublin and Navan. In this photograph taken in 1912, this group of cyclists from the Irish Road Club were surveying the course for their 100 Mile competition. The cyclists all sport modern looking 'safety' bicycles. There is also a tandem cycle, a type that was particularly popular with touring cyclists.

IRISH ROAD CLUB 'ONE HUNDRED' 1912

During the 1912 Irish Road Club 'Hundred', the club's treasurer, EP Monks, who was third on handicap, gets a 'push-off' from a willing helper while TWM's son Thomas Desmond looks on.

Ralph Mecredy rounds the corner at Balrath
Cross Roads during the Irish Road Club
'Hundred'. Mecredy, a son of 'Arjay'
Mecredy, the proprietor of *The Irish Cyclist*,
was aboard the Lusitania when it was torpe-
doed off Cork in 1915 and survived by
swimming ashore.

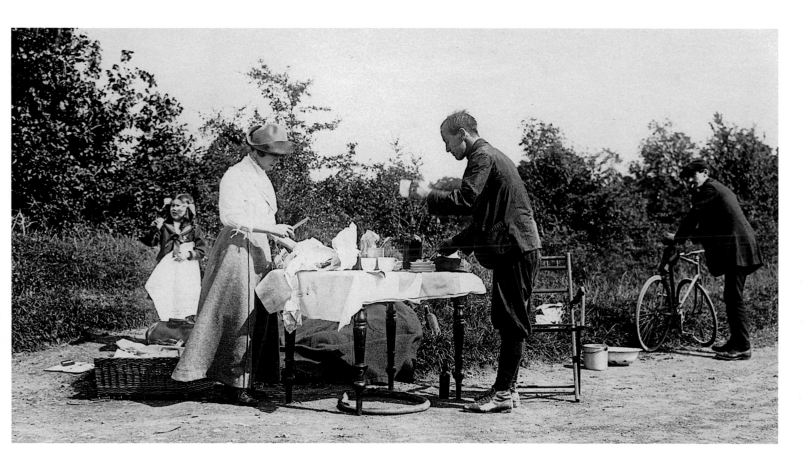

Welcome refreshment. F Guy of Belfast, the holder of the Irish 100 miles record, partakes of some welcome refreshment at Balrath Crossroads during the 1912 event.

HAWKER'S CRASH AT LOUGHSHINNY

In 1913 The Daily Mail offered a prize of £5,000 for a circuit of Great Britain. The course of 1,540 miles was divided into nine stages, one of which was from Oban in Scotland to Dublin. Three entries were received including one from the Sopwith Company for its test pilot, Harry Hawker. Having refuelled at Larne, Hawker headed for the Dublin control. While still a short distance away his engine started to lose power, possibly due to broken valve springs, and Hawker decided to alight on the water at Loughshinny to investigate. Unfortunetly, at a critical moment his foot slipped off the rudder pedal (due to grease on his shoe) with the result that a wingtip struck the sea wrecking the plane. Hawker scrambled from the wreckage unhurt but his passenger, Harry Kauper, of the Sopwith Company needed to be taken to hospital with a cut head and a broken arm. Very sportingly, The Daily Mail gave Hawker £1,000 for his gallant effort.

The first photograph, (facing page), shows efforts to tow the wreckage in to shore, while in the second (above) the seaplane's broken floats are surrounded by a curious crowd.

THE KILDARE HUNT CLUB MEETING AT PUNCHESTOWN 1912

The motor car was not long in replacing the horse and carriage at social occasions such as the Kildare Hunt Club Meeting at Punchestown.

Mr Walter Summers of Marlay, Rathfarnham, and his party leaving the enclosure of the Irish Automobile Club.

The growth in ownership of motor cars by 1912 is amply
demonstrated by the number of cars in the Irish
Automobile Club enclosure for its members – all parked
cloely together. Meetings at Punchestown were major
social events where one paraded in one's best clothes.

Quite what this woman is offering is unclear –
perhaps she's a programme seller.

ROWING AT ISLANDBRIDGE

The River Liffey at Islandbridge has long been a popular
venue for boat races and here a well-turned out crew is seen
under way. Its not clear if this is a training run or a race but
one would expect more evidence of spectators for a race.

TOLKA BRIDGE, DRUMCONDRA

The start of a motorcycle competition from just north of Tolka Bridge, Drumcondra, Dublin. This was the starting point for many cycle races and later as interest grew in motorcycles, for motorcycle competitions.

An unidentified competitor starting his Douglas motorcycle at the same location. Douglas was a British motorcycle manufacturer between 1907 and 1957 based in Bristol. Horiziontally opposed twin cylinder engines were a feature of their motorcycles and between 1913 and 1922 they also manufactured a range of cars.

MURATTI TROPHY COMPETITION

One of the most important motorcycle competitions was for the Muratti
Trophy. This magnificent silver trophy had been presented to the Motorcycle
Union of Ireland in 1904. The competition took the form of a reliability trial
and took place over two days. The photograph shows one of the competitors
in the 1909 contest, OC Godfrey on his Rex, leaving the Dublin control.

THE ROYAL VISIT OF 1911

Of all TW Murphy's surviving photographs it is his photographs of the Royal Visit by King George V and Queen Mary in 1911 that have the greatest power to startle and surprise. The visit was part of George Vs accession tour, (having been crowned just a fortnight earlier) and he was greeted with such enthusiasm that it was suggested that he might have solved the crisis over Home Rule at a stroke. Such optimism proved tragically unfounded but there was no denying the fevour with which the majority of Irish people welcomed the King and Queen Mary. From our viewpoint it is the events surrounding Easter week 1916 that colour our understanding of that decade but clearly, as these photographs show, there is more.

Home Rule for Ireland was the burning issue of the day but there was also a real and genuine enthusism for the Royal Visit as witnessed by the extrodinary numbers of people who thronged the streets of Dublin with the one aim of catching a glimpse of the royal couple. Dublin may have been a city of great contrasts, between rich and poor and between Unionist and Nationalist, but the vast majority welcomed the 1911 visit wholeheartetly.

That eye for the unusual, the candid, of TWM is again in evidence in his photographs of the Royal visit – the royal couple's luggage being carried ashore, the top-hatted Dubliner face-to-face with a policeman, the couple on bycycles passing a guard-of-honour and the trams full of excited people heading for Phoenix Park and the troop review– all bring a new perspective to our understanding of the Royal Visit.

TW Murphy's photographs illustrate this fervour in a way no other photographs of this event that I have seen manage to convey, while giving a sense of a way of life about to disappear.

George R. I.

THE ROYAL VISIT OF 1911

King George V and Queen Alexandra and their party arrived
in Kingstown (now Dun laoghaire) on the evening of July 7th
in the Royal Yachts Victoria & Albert and Alexandra escorted
by the cruisers Cochrane and Carnarvon as well as ships from
the Home Fleet.

The Lord Lieutenant of Ireland, Lord Aberdeen and Lady
Aberdeen were among the many dignitaries at Kingstown to
welcome the Royal Party.

The Royal Party landed on Irish soil at 10.30 am on
the 8th July and then travelled by open horse-drawn
coach to Dublin Castle in brilliant sunshine.

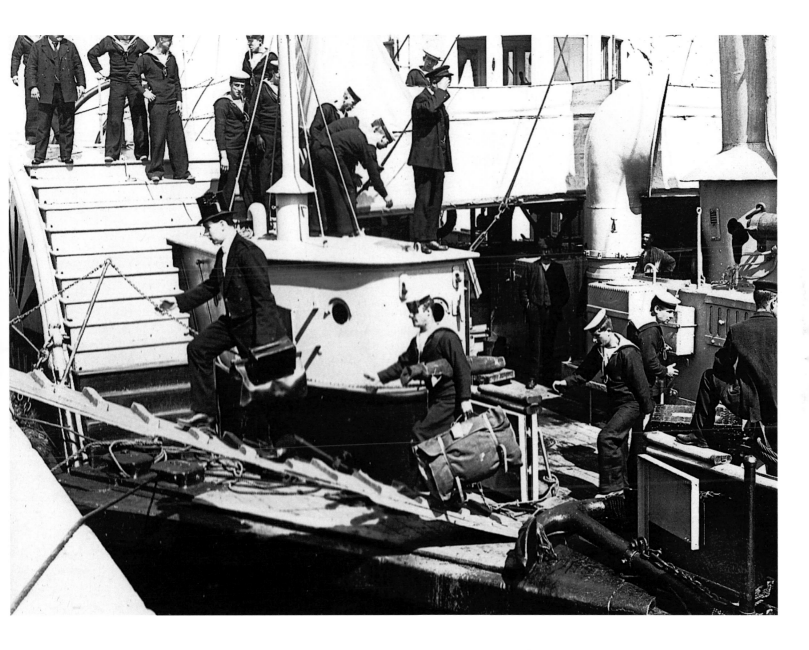

No less than eight vans followed the king and queen carrying their personal luggage. Here the first of this luggage comes ashore.

The route from Kingstown to Dublin Castle was lined with men from the Royal Navy and Royal Marines. At Leeson Street Bridge, an ornate gate to the city had been erected with signs proclaiming 'Welcome to our ancient city'.

The Royal Party were led into Dublin by the 8th Royal Hussars on horseback, seen here making their way through the throngs of people who lined the route in many places.

Large crowds gathered along the entire route to Dublin Castle, eagerly awaiting, as here at College Green, their first glimpse of the royal couple.

The numbers of people visible in TW Murphy's photographs who turned out to cheer or simply to see the Royal Party is quite staggering. It is hard to imagine that this apparently loyal city just five years later would be home to a bloody armed insurrection, yet such was the case. This tightly packed crowd is close to the entrance to Dublin Castle.

Another view of College Green and the viewing stand outside the
Bank of Ireland building, formally the seat of the Irish parliament prior
to the Act of Union.

Crowds throng the street outside Trinity College at the junction with College Green. To a modern eye the crowds are astonishing and contain a high proportion of military men.

Another photograph of the scene outside Dublin Castle, this time of the main entrance through which the royal party will shortly pass.

Several members of King's Council (Silks) in full regalia cross the yard of Dublin Castle while awaiting the arrival of the Royal party.

A charming photograph of a member of the Dublin Metropolitan police and a Dubliner, dressed in his best for the occasion.

Dublin's finest. Members of the Dublin Metropolitan Police and a single Royal Irish Constabulary constable parade on Ormond Quay. Note the varying styles of moustache displayed by all except one clean-shaven individual..

The Rolls-Royce of Dr. Oliver St. John Gogarty photographed in Grafton Street, bedecked with flags for the occasion, and where the people are awaiting the arrival of the Royal party. St. John Gogarty was a noted Rolls-Royce enthusiast.

Crowded trams taking people to the Review of Troops in
Dublin's Phoenix Park pass along the city quays.

A review of troops took place in the Phoenix Park, where the King, mounted on horseback took the salute.

This unfortunate is receiving medical attention after being thrown from his horse. Another photograph of the incident would suggest that he had his leg broken by the fall.

While the mounted soldiers await the passage of the Royal Party, a cycling couple pass their ordered ranks.

Crowd stream through the main gates of the Phoenix Park, specially decorated for the occasion, on their way to the royal review due to take place on the 'Forty Acres'. All forms of transport are visible – bicycles, cars horse-drawn vehicles and a tram – in the brilliant sunshine that illuminated the royal visit.

A photograph that more than any other conveys the
excitement and bustle of Dublin streets during the visit.
Save for a few constables, everyone is hurrying in one
direction while the passengers on top of the tram crane
to see some activity out of sight of the photographer.

A locomotive bedecked with flowers in anticipation of pulling the Royal visitors train to Maynooth where, in their only journey outside Dublin, they visited the college.

The busy scene at the junction of College Green and Grafton Street shortly after
the Royal party had passed and normal tram and horse-drwn traffic re-asserts
itself.

THE DUBLIN HORSE SHOW

Activity outside the main entrance of the Royal Dublin Society showground's during Horse Show week. Motor cars quickly became popular amongst Irish society were given status by the use by the Lord Lieutenant to travel in them to such events.

A motorist drives into the grounds of the Royal Dublin Society at Ballsbridge.

Dr Glenn, a well–known pioneer motorist, and his
party arrive by car at the Dublin Horse Show.

High fashion in the show-ground's of the Royal Dublin Society during the Dublin Horse Show.

Awaiting activity in the show-ring, this photograph also
shows the velo-drome cycle track that ran around the edge
of the ring, and which was the scene of many exciting and
important cycle races.

'A sea of umbrellas' at the same area of the RDS. Ireland's ever-changeable weather, it seems, was just as unpredictable in 1912 when this photograph was taken.

At the height of its popularity in 1912, the Dublin Horse Show was a 'must' for Irish society to see and be seen.

THE DUBLIN TO BELFAST AIR RACE 1912

In 1912, the Irish Aero Club, stung by suggestions that it had done little to promote the growth of aviation in Ireland since its foundation in November 1909, organised an air race from Dublin to Belfast. The race started from Leopardstown racecourse and the four starters encounted very strong head winds right from the start. Before long, all four had been forced to land with Jimmy Valentine landing near Newry to establish a new distance record for Ireland. Because of the high winds the race was abandoned. However, a large crowd had gathered at Balmoral showgrounds where the finish of the race was expected. Because the crowd had been disappointed, several of the aviators undertook to put on a display of flying on the following weekend, an event that was to end in tragedy with the death of the British aviator Astley.

James Valentine talks to Astley beside Valentine's Deperdussin in the Balmoral showgrounds.

Watched by his manager, Astley prepares to take-off in his Bleriot monoplane. Because of the small space available in the Balmoral showgrounds, the helpers are restraining the plane while its engine runs up to full power in an effort to shorten the take-off run.

Astley airborne over the show grounds in his
Bleriot monoplane.

Valentine in the cockpit of his Deperdussin about to take-off.

Jimmy Valentine makes ready for take-off in his Deperdussin monoplane. In the race a week earlier he had set a new Irish distance record by flying non-stop from Dublin to Newry, landing with difficulty in a small field two miles from the town.

Valentine, Salmet and Astley pose for a photograph together.
Within half an hour Astley would be dead, having suffered an
engine problem while in flight, and turning into the ground
to avoid crashing into the crowd.

Valentine leaves the Balmoral show grounds in his
Gregorie car. Pilots of the day were a mix of pioneers and
showmen, who often depended on income from public
appearances to enable them to continue flying.

THE IRISH ROAD CLUB INVITATION 'FIFTY' 1911

The doyen of Irish cyclists, RJ Mecredy, editor of *The Irish Cyclist* and the *Motor News,* photographed at the annual Irish Road Club Invitation 'Fifty' cycle race. Mecredy is on the right and centre is AJ Sweeney, one of the event timekeepers.

A rider starts out on the Navan Road under the watchful eye of RJ Mecredy. Mecredy had been the sensational winner of the British 1 mile, 5 mile, 10 mile and 25 mile championships in 1890, riding a bicycle fitted with John Boyd Dunlop's pneumatic tyres.

One of the competitors passes through a small hamlet on the Navan course. The 1911 event was won by a Scottish rider, J Miller from Larkhall, the first time a Scot had competed in the event. The winner covered the course from Dublin to Navan and back in two hours 36 minutes and 35 seconds.

TRICYCLE TIME TRIAL

Tricycles remained very popular amongst cyclists well into the 1900's and here we see the start of a time trial between two riders mounted on tricycles at an unidentified location.

CYCLE TOURING

Cycling as a pastime had boomed in the late 1800s and on any weekend the roads were filled with cycling groups touring the countryside as well as participating in time trials. Cycling brought a new freedom to people and an opportunity to travel easily beyond their immediate surroundings.

A group of touring cyclists in County Wicklow. Interest in cycling peaked about 1890 when it was given further impetus by the invention of the pneumatic tyre by Belfast veterinarian John Boyd Dunlop. The cycling boom provided a freedom of travel ordinary people had now known before and cycle clubs sprang up all over the country.

The same group of touring cyclists seem to be making free with the staff of this hotel.

HEADS!

It's heads down to solve a problem on this bicycle. The
cyclists are all members of the Anfield Club visiting the Irish
Road Club Invitation 'Fifty' on the Navan Road.

TOURING MOTORCYCLISTS

A group of motorcyclists, including in the background several with
sidecars, pause for a group photograph. The occasion may have been
a motorcycle competition rather than a touring group.

ROSSLARE SAND RACES 1913

Sand racing was a popular form of competition in motorsport's early days and races were held in Ireland at Portmarnock, Duncannon, Rosslare, Magilligan and in Kerry. Speeds were surprisingly high and at Rosslare ST Robinson driving a Talbot was timed at 107mph, a very high speed given the unpredictable nature of the surface.

In the first photograph two cars are about to start on the railway sleepers laid down in the sand to give them traction when setting off.

A 25hp Talbot and a Daimler about to set off in the 4-mile race.

TAKING WOUNDED SOLDIERS FROM THE PORTS

A large number of wounded soldiers, many of them Irish, were brought to Ireland during the Great War to convalesce. The Irish Automobile Club's members organised an ambulance service to transport them from the ports to their destinations. In this photograph, a Daimler car, driven by Sir Horace Plunkett, prepares to set off with wounded soilders aboard. Sir Horace Plunkett was the founder of the Irish Agricultural Organisation Society and was President of the Irish Automobile Club.

Another IAC car leaves Dublin port with a compliment of wounded. In 1918 the IAC was awarded the 'Royal' prefix to its title, becoming the Royal Irish Automobile Club, in recognition of the humanitarian services by its members during the conflict.

THE PARNELL MONUMENT

Newly erected in 1911 when this photograph was taken, the monument to Charles Stewart Parnell, had come about through the efforts of John Redmond, leader of the Parnellite element of the Irish parliamentary Party when it split following Parnell's death in 1891. He raised funds to erect a suitable monument to Parnell at the northern end of Dublin's O'Connell Street, choosing the American Augustus Saint Gaudens to sculpt the statue.

THE GOUGH MEMORIAL

Field Marshal Hugh Gough, 1st Viscount Gough (1779-1869) was born at Woodstown House, County Limerick, into an Anglo-Irish family long settled in County Limerick since the early 17th century. He had a long and successful career in the British Army and was said to have commanded more actions that any other general save Wellington.

The Gough Memorial was sited in Dublin's Phoenix Park, but was blown up in 1957.

DUBLIN CITY HALL

In the year 1761, the Merchants of Dublin formed themselves into a society, and seven years later in 1768, the society advertised an architectural competition for the design of a new exchange building to be erected on a site at Cork Hill, previously occupied by the church of Sainte Marie del Dame. The competition attracted a total of 61 entries and was won by the architect, Thomas Cooley. Construction began in 1769 and the new exchange was completed ten years later in 1779. The Royal Exchange, or City Hall as it is now known, is one of Dublin's finest and most sophisticated 18th century buildings.

Two photographs of Dublin's imposing City Hall sits
on a sloping site facing Parliament Street.

THE ROYAL NORTH OF IRELAND YACHT CLUB 1909

98 The annual hill-climb of the North of Ireland Yacht Club was
held over a private road at Cultra, just outside Belfast, and is
today the site of the Ulster Folk and Transport Museum, who in
recent years have revived the event. The Club's fine clubhouse
on the shores of Belfast Lough was the event's headquarters.

NEWRY

A tranquil scene at Newry, County Down.

CYCLE RACING AT THE JONES'S ROAD CINDER TRACK

At the height of the cycle boom in the 1880s a cinder track was
installed at Jones's Road in Dublin. It was to prove the site of many
outstanding races and was also used as a running track.

The final of the 1912 Quarter-mile GAA Championship at the Freeman's Journal staff sports. R Lynch of the Harp Cycle Club on the outside is the winner with PJ Sheridan of Kilcock just inches behind.

A delightful photograph of a lady motorcyclist preparing to go touring
in County Wicklow. Lady motorcyclists were comparitivly rare in
Irleand, although lady cyclists abounded.

The Swift car of RJ Mecredy is dwarfed by a char-a-banc outside the Royal Hotel at Glendalough. Glendalough was a very popular destination for outings of groups from Dublin and char-a-banc's were often to be seen on the road leading there. The char-a-banc's were the forerunner of the modern bus but lacked the weather protection buses would provide.

A varied selection of travellers and their vehicles gather outside the
Royal Hotel, Glendalough in County Wicklow. There is a small car
- a Swift - a motorcycle with wicker sidecar, a larger touring car
with an enclosed cabin and open back seats and a char-a-banc
capable of taking around twenty passengers.

IN THE FURRY GLEN

A well-known Dublin trader, W Curtis, the managing director of Messrs. Yeates & Son, photographed at the wheel of his B.S.A. car in the Furry Glen in Dublin's Phoenix Park. This was a favourite place for TW Murphy to take such photographs.

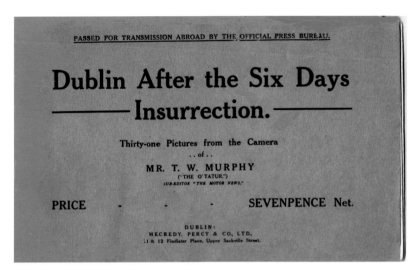

Dublin After the Six Days ——— Insurrection. ———

Thirty-one Pictures from the Camera
.. of ..
MR. T. W. MURPHY
("THE O'TATUR.")
SUB-EDITOR "THE MOTOR NEWS."

PRICE   -   -   -   SEVENPENCE Net.

DUBLIN:
MECREDY, PERCY & CO., LTD.,
11 & 12 Findlater Place, Upper Sackville Street.

The 'O'Tatur' was TWM's pen name – a 'Murphy' being a slang name for a potato.

THE 1916 RISING

In utter contrast to TWM's photographs taken just five years earlier of the royal visit of George V to Dublin are his photographs of the aftermath of the 1916 Rising. Looking at the ruined streets and destroyed buildings at the very heart of Dublin it is hard to reconcile the excited, cheering crowds that thronged the streets just five short years earlier. As always, TWM's eye caught the unusual and amid all the devastation are images of nuns feeding the poor; a soldier rescued from the ruins of a collapsed building; a republician prisoner captured and being marched away under escort; soldiers at rest in the grounds of the Provost's House in Trinity College and, a sign of the adaptability of mankind, a newspaper seller outside the ruins of the GPO.

TWM's photographs were in demand and were reproduced in at least three publications and down the years several have appeared un-attributed in many subsequent publications. His employers, Mecredy Percy Limited, published *Dublin after the Six Days Insurrection – thirty-one pictures from the camera of Mr. TW Murphy ("The O'Tatur") sub-editor of* The Motor News, price sevenpence. Each of the thirty-one photographs is reproduced full-page and in excellent quality. At the same time Messrs Hely's of Dame Street, Dublin, published *The Sinn Féin Revolt Illustrated* containing a large number of TWM's photographs and at least one other London based publication published his photographs of the Rising.

The majority of the photographs are of the devestation caused by the shelling of central Dublin and by the fighting that went on there but as with TWM's photographs of the Royal Visit it is the other more candid photographs that bring the tragedy to life and open a newwindow to the events of Easter week 1916.

Henry Street, from the west side, looking towards Nelson's Pillar, with the shell of the General Post Office nearest it on the right. The barricades that blocked this street have been cleared in this photograph.

Sackville Street, now O'Connell Street, seen from one of the
houses on the west side. The level of destruction is well illustrated
in this photograph as the populace turns out to view the
destruction at the heart of their city

Another view of the north side of the General Post Office, now no more than a shell. This building was, of course, the focal point of some of the fiercest fighting during the Rising, and the key target of shelling by the British gunboat on the River Liffey.

Hopkin's Corner, a well-known landmark, on Eden Quay,
totally destroyed.

On Wednesday May 6th two soldiers who had originally been prisoners in the GPO were discovered amongst the ruins of the Coliseum Theatre in Henry Street. They had been freed when the interior of the GPO was in flames and had hidden there as they believed the fighting was still going on.

Workmen start to remove the debris of fallen buildings from Middle
Abbey Street. The authorities, having destroyed the centre of the city,
now worked quickly to remove the results of their work.

A Sisters of Charity nun feeding hungry boys during
the Rising. The fighting and subsequent shelling of the city
centre imposed great hardship on many ordinary people,
inhabitants of the inner city.

Several nuns of the Sisters of Charity order photographed while they distributed much needed food to the poor. Like other European cities at the time, Dublin had a large population in its centre and little thought seems to have been given to their welfare as the authorities sought to put down the Rising.

The military stand guard at the entrance to Trinity College.
Trinity College was not seen as important by those that
planned the Rising but by Tuesday it held a strong force of
regular army units and became the main base for the
Imperial forces.

A volunteer, identifiable by the lighter colour of his uniform, stands guard on the ruins of the GPO.

Regular soldiers march past volunteers on duty at the
ruins of the GPO.

A prisoner is taken away into captivity under an armed escort.

As a result of damage to the gas mains on the bridge over the
River Liffey at Sackville Street there was a gas explosion. Repairs
are under way in TW Murphy's photograph.

Units of the regular army occupied the house of the Provost of
Trinity College. Trinity College formed one end of a line of
bases stretching to Kingsbridge station that, by the Wednesday
after the Rising, effectively cut the Republican forces in two.

Liberty Hall, the offices of the Irish Transport and General Workers Union, was taken over as headquarters for the Citizen Army, and as a result was heavily bombarded by the British forces.

Crowds of Dubliners watch the destruction of a dangerous building
on Eden Quay.

Troops guard the railway bridge at the Clontarf Road that
carried the vital rail link with the north of the country.

Prisoners being conveyed to the boats for deportation to
prison camp in Wales.

Civilian ambulances lined up for a review by General Maxwell at the Royal Barracks. (now Collins Barracks). In the background can be seen the gun turrets of three of the Rolls-Royce armoured cars used by the authorities to help put down the Rising.

A second view of the ambulances in the Royal Barracks. These
ambulances played an invaluable role, collecting nationalist,
civilian and military wounded without distinction.

And life returns to normal. A paper seller returns to his 'spot' outside the ruins of the GPO.

LIST OF PHOTOGRAPHS

Oswald Pilningham: 1907